Hitch

NIGHTWOOD EDITIONS · 2006
GIBSONS LANDING, BC

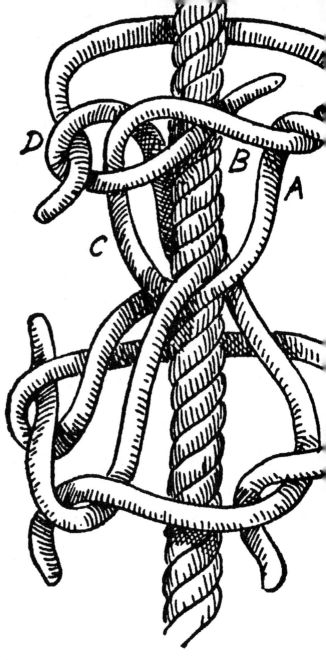

Hitch

MATTHEW HOLMES

Nightwood Editions
773 Cascade Crescent
Gibsons, BC
Canada V0N 1V9

Edited by Silas White
Typeset in Bell MT Standard by Carleton Wilson
Interior design by Matthew Holmes and Carleton Wilson
Cover design by Carleton Wilson

Semaphore images are taken from *Navy and International Code Flag Cards: A Product of the U.S. Naval Training Device Center.*
Knot images are taken from *Knots, Splices, and Rope Work* by A. Hyatt Verrill (New York: The Norman W. Henley Publishing Co., 1917).

We gratefully acknowledge the support of the Canada Council for the Arts and the British Columbia Arts Council for our publishing program.

Canada Council   Conseil des Arts
for the Arts   du Canada

BRITISH
COLUMBIA
ARTS COUNCIL
Supported by the Province of British Columbia

Printed and bound in Canada.

LIBRARY AND ARCHIVES CANADA CATALOGUING IN PUBLICATION

Holmes, Matthew, 1977–
    Hitch / Matthew Holmes.

Poems.

"A blewointment book".

ISBN 0-88971-214-X

    I. Title.

PS8565.O6365H58 2006   C811'.6   C2006-901487-6

for beth—

9   at a certain point, Degas

I. A SCIENCE EVERY DAY

13   hotel again
14   Smith's Invisible Hand
16   Heisenberg's Uncertainty Principle
18   Avogadro's Law
20   Baer's Law (I and II)
22   Starling's Law of the Heart
24   redshadow poems
26   hotel (after the flood)

II. BEFORE OTHERS ARE THERE

29   buckshot fullstop
30   iodine
32   Honesty
33   a moose running along the highway
        outside Memramcook
34   a moveable
35   orts: February evening
36   traditional dances for tourists
37   the tension of love and windows
38   trans-Canada

III. GREEN TOMATOES

41   tying the river
43   to beth, sleeping
44   beth seeking poems
46   ghazal of July storm
47   green tomatoes
48   Belgrave Avenue
50   Samuel Marchbanks' daughter
51   Piazza del Nettuno
52   confessions of a zucchini painter
53   dog show blues
54   the life and evolution of dust bunnies
55   a local history of the air conditioner
56   the trials and exile of fridges
58   to the poet who stole my boots, my poem.

IV. COAL SMOKE DREAMS

61 morning crow ghazal
62 woodpeckers
63 walking Dallas Road
64 three pumpkins
65 Oaxaca potato
66 Mazinaw/Bon Echo
68 entropy
69 spring this year
70 queen jane approximately
71 fall
72 the reliquaries of trees
73 owl shaped in reeds

V. HITCH

77 fig. 1: preface
78 fig. 2: the premise of tying
79 fig. 3: tying the knot
80 fig. 4: hagiography
81 fig. 5: mooring
82 fig. 6: aeromancy
83 fig. 7: chains
84 fig. 8: editing
85 fig. 9: alphabet
86 fig. 10: fast
87 fig. 11: coming together
88 fig. 12: pause
89 fig. 13: stranded
90 fig. 14: June

92 Notes on the poems
94 Acknowledgements
96 About the author

CONTENTS

AT A CERTAIN POINT, DEGAS
for RW

at a certain point, Degas
put aside his pictures of French ballerinas looking over their
    shoulders
and found dark love in the shape of horses' flight.

someone handed him photographs of these beasts in air—
an American's bet played within a paddock
lined behind by a wall of time
to chart their gallop, their weightlessness
known only, and briefly, to this cameraman
and to the ranks who eased into underbellies
with pointed pike before being crushed by the cavalry.

this line, this line into a horse's stomach
is what he was after: with a clutch of damp clay like shit
he fixed a horse flying into hardness,
a horse stretching between the blinks of a thousand races—
suspended by copper wire, he impaled it,
embedded a skeleton, made it an axis of disembowelling,
an art of arched backs and legs pulled tight.

knifed into the moment, that flash of horse flight,
within speed and clop of hoof, inside the time of midsection,
there is a way to stop things:
a writing on glass,
a spine sculpted vertically into brass,
a measurement for all horses in the nose-length of losing
a finishing line.

This poem intentionally blank.

I. A SCIENCE EVERY DAY

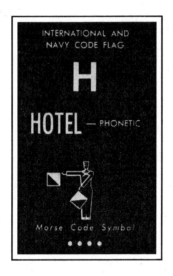

HOTEL AGAIN

outside, the E of "HOTEL"
shines my window blue and hum.

where my watch was, a darkroom smell,
the skin there light and fixed.

evangelism on television, a science every day
reveals the word as cheque and balance.

in my drawer, *Gideon's*; on the armoire, a *Digest*,
and the city outside saying sin, sin, sin if you can.

the rolling boom of an elevator door, the heave
of an edgeless bed; cool croissants in the morning.

The neighbours didn't know Smith very well. He was always so quiet. When he got home he had the record on by six (if things were running smoothly) and he'd wait a second, listening for that slip of vinyl turning before the song had started, that faint crackle taking on the sound of the traffic, white and rushing outside. He walked into the kitchen where the song, just starting, was already lost in the roll of wheels on asphalt, like water over the round backs of pebbles, seeping through the window and into his space. He opened the cupboard. Pulled out a glass and bottle, the Macallan, slung it loosely from its neck as he moved back into the hall, through that middle space where record mixed with traffic again, and into the centre room where the music was. Lenny Breau spinning chords. Smith readied himself for sadness. Quick looks into the mirror; quick looks away. Let his shoulders slump a bit. He thought about the people he hadn't written, and how long. He thought of friends who had reinvented themselves. He thought about the last time he'd seen them, where that was. When. When they gave up their life here and moved to a farm near the ocean, where they watched the sun, learnt the seasons, wrote letters that sounded so false from who they'd been before, signed the same names to them. He thought about how they had changed themselves just by thinking it, as though who they were, and where, were options. He couldn't decide on what was true. But his neighbours knew nothing of this. In the morning, say, or taking out his keys with cold fingers, he'd exchange with them those neighbourly things that neighbours exchange. Saying hello like it was some sort of currency—the local one, not American—that they'd each hand the other over the little fence between their front-door landings, the one the mailman always sidled over. Little currencies going up and down in value, measured against the weather and the headlines, traded and priced over hedge and rusted handrail. Bright and polished little stones. These things that let you know you were in a good place, that you were good. At worst, he said a simple hello, a nod with the right amount of buoyancy in his brow, enough not to be closed. They knew Smith from this: that he was a nice man. But they couldn't hear him when the record was playing. Inside, the guitar's fretboard was holding onto his breathing, not tightly but firm enough, like a fistful of sand; the strum and pause of the chords stroked his temple, moved the hair out of his face, topped up his glass for him; and the harmonics, pure and ringing out into the quiet of the song like that, into the apartment, almost unseen, were tearing at him with strong fingers, clawing his resolve into pieces, making it hurt.

When he graduated from making phony lost dog posters, Werner didn't even realize it had happened. He'd been walking back with a coffee from Magnolia's, stepping around a couple looking at one of his flyers—*How terrible; can you imagine; a Christmas puppy; in this cold*—and thought to himself (with the white noise of a mild hangover trailing him) how he'd go about it if he found a bag stuffed with cash. There's not a lot of it moving around these days, especially if it's in large bills. And what are you supposed to do—really—what is the Good Citizen supposed to do? Does the city's website have something on it? Do they really expect you to notify the cops? Or maybe run after that guy ahead of you on the sidewalk and say—*Excuse me, did you drop this huge fucking Ziploc™ packed with hundreds?* He'd thought about giving Tracy a call. Werner was seeing two sisters: Triny and Tracy. Tracy knew he made the posters for kicks but Triny was a bit tricky. She'd discovered a pile of posters once when she was over—all of them for different pets—and he'd had to do some quick thinking to explain why he had them, and why they all had his number on them. Now she thought he was this neighbourhood hero: the organized mind taking on the area's soaring have-you-seen-Bobo rates, helping all these local families catatonic with worry. It was about this time that he started working on a new kind of poster, and the first call came a couple of weeks later—*Yeah, hi, is this the organized crime guy that put the posters up? I found your cash, yeah, over on Euclid Ave. Listen, I know you said you couldn't offer a reward, but I'm stuck. . . and I want half, alright? I'll give it back to you, but I need half*—so Werner made the arrangements and met the guy and the guy handed him a baggie of cash, no questions. This went on for quite some time. Every week or two there'd be a call: someone else trying to return some money they said they'd found, always looking for a cut. He'd go out and meet them and they'd hand over this fucking grab bag. He had no idea, really, but it started to get a bit dull it was so regular. The only uncertainty was how much they'd give him: a couple thou, ten, often more. The numbers stopped meaning that much to Werner; relativity kicking in. He stopped reading the news, stopped showing up at work. Started planning a little trip with one of the sisters. Which sister was the only thing—the one that knew or the one that didn't. And only once, since this whole thing had started, did he get a call about a dog—but he told her, this woman with the hope in her voice, to keep it, he didn't need it, and hung up.

AVOGADRO'S LAW

Contrary to how Science still tells the story, Avogadro was no
great chemist. Actually, he spied for the yankees (fronting as
a clam diver off the Mexican coast) during the revolt against
the Spanish. It was there, in the curve of the Gulf, watching
the bay over the stone lip of the breakwater, spooning green
butter from an avocado and pasting it with his tongue onto the
roof of his mouth, that he took his name and found his home.
Science will tell you that he was an Italian with a propensity
for hams and yelling at people when he was feeling sociable.
That he would sit on his front porch under the grape trellis
on Wednesdays. That he was a man obsessed with the secret
lives of gases, with invisible measurements. Some of this may
be similar to his true life: squinting into the space between the
horizon, trying to find a fault in its line, to focus just past its
tectonic curve; or knowing the bubbling of a clam under the
sand, twenty feet below, for what it was. As for the volume of
gases, there was really only the one attempt when young to
bottle his own and send it, wrapped and ribboned, to the father
of a girl who was not allowed to play with him anymore. Much
later, after the signing of the Guadalupe Hidalgo and half of
Mexico gone, Avogadro retired, stayed on in Mexico to eat

great amounts of mole poblano, chilies and chocolate mixing with the mescal in him, building up pressure. In the mid-autumn, the evenings had a comfortable cool heat from the air off the water, and he would lie in his hammock counting, always counting. He would count the shots of mescal it took him to lose count, though no one now can agree on how many this was. He'd count the lines of lampblack stained into his fingertips from his drawing pen, the ridges of skin like currents of water on a map. He'd count the distinctiveness of each chili he could taste under the slide of thick, melted chocolate, rolling his tongue slowly like he was searching for the words: *six, ten, twenty-three*. . . . And the locals would roll their eyes, say, *Here's Señor Avo full of gases again,* not believing that a gringo, however long he'd been there, could count something that small, that blended, so much a part of their tastes, so much a part of everything else it was mixed with. Laughter and another round. *Twenty-three,* he would announce, knowing where he was, figuring one thing was equal to another out here, looking out at the lights from the ironclads shining in Brownsville, and between him and them, the Gulf, black as carbon.

What's important here, what's true, is not so much what happened but why. When he reached Petersburg and found them gone, Baer went on to Siberia, hired a small barge in Yakutsk and travelled north along the Lena, scanning the banks, pacing the decks. Of course it was foolish to expect to find them: by the time their name was known to the world their exile was already in place. And in place, in politics, in pulse, even, the Decembrists were already somewhere else. Their hunger and consumption shifted to the nurturing glances of small men with stained overcoats and questionable poetics, to the sudden embarrassments of epileptics, to hidden sardine tins, to the early-morning rhythm of breadmakers and their simple allegiances to primary colours. The spirit was dormant. But for Baer there was something down under the mantle, shouldering through the water table, feeding off pickings from the teeth of stalactites, sleeping under palaces and castles, uneasy. A feeling that some place, some person could have it. Baer needed to smell the scent off it before it was. Needed time to move faster, to know where it was going, to be able to recall himself as being a part of it once it had come and gone. But the deck rocked slightly as the water's pace quickened, and still nothing. The shore started to rise above them, leaving a dark stain on the walls of their peripheral vision. The damp of the rock shone. And something. Baer held up his hand, pointed them over to the right bank where it was carved into the cliff-rock. His foot sank into the muck there. If they looked up they would see that the sky was cold and mottled, serrated by the turf at the eroded edge of the rise. But they watched him. In the muddiness of a back eddy in the rocks he stooped and picked up what he'd seen from the water. He held it close and his clothes bled with the wet of it. In his arms he held a tight blue fist of a child, not yet born, aborted, looking like the history of all mammals, smelling like the bend in a river. Baer walked with it to where the barge swung, up to his hips in water. He looked past the crew with their dull Mongolian stares, told the captain to turn the boat around. That was what happened.

1.

When S— was eleven, living in V—, he found a bird sidled into the crack between the old brick sidewalk and the lean of someone's retaining wall. It was a chick, blinking at the low world sideways, lower than it had ever been. It would not fly. S— had been told about mites and could imagine the tear in his finger its beak would make, where the dirt would mix into his blood and when he was twenty-two or so, like a splinter left in too long, make its way to his heart and stop it. So he made a sort of funnel out of paper, scooped up the bird without touching it and brought it home, where it sat in a shoebox in his window for three days before dying.

2.

In V—, later, S— would go out to the pier and stand listening to the sound of the pebble beach rolling itself in the flowtide: a sound of slot machines, rainsticks, popcorn, knuckles cracking, oak leaves. In the cold, his ears would start to pierce his thoughts, then numb, then ache deep inside his head. The mist bringing the broken stumps of pilings around the pier into a sharper presence, like the buildup to surprise. When the pulse knows before the throat does.

3.

She told him once that she came from a star whose light hadn't reached us yet. There. Right below Orion's belt, pointing. Just before dawn with a cargo train rolling by, rolling by, rolling by in the fields outside of T—. The morning she left, both of them quiet with it. The sky getting that sharp blue colour. Trying to sense how emptiness can give the feeling of weight. Like water.

4.

His ring said 92.5 on the inside: sterling. He took it off his finger and sniffed the lighter skin there. Not paying attention. The ring bounced once on his desk and he came out of it— wherever he'd just been. Put the ring back on. Outside, winter was coming, the rain on the mud on the other side of the road making it silver, like snow was already collecting in the low places. Inside, the hiss of the air was on, circulating something warm through the building. Down the street he could see a few people in other offices: standing at their windows, walking by. Each building housing its own season, opposite to the one outside. Each person somewhere else, or in another time.

REDSHADOW POEMS

Our earth's shadow is always red but we never see it. . .
— THE GLOBE AND MAIL

like strata
loam clay mantle
star

•

the earth's red shadows
the blue sapped out of the sun
and sunsets left circling the planet,

looking for a way to rise
and leave

•

this world bends its sunsets
around oceans.
glutted on blue from the sun,
it sends out shadows, red,
behind it, unseen

•

as the sunset is bent
pinned by horizon to sky

its shadows haemorrhaging
into night

•

it leaks
wine poured in the dark

•

some write they wish on the light of dead stars,

time broken with the idea of waiting that long

to see; behind us we leave a stain of dark

unnoticed

•

refracting the sunset, the curve continues
its descent

shadows turn from the ocean

•

the constant outward shadow moving
past the moon (no longer red)

giving space more colour

than before our sun rose

HOTEL (AFTER THE FLOOD)

consider the beer-can tab I almost swallowed tonight:
I can still feel it in my throat, where it would be if it had
    lodged there

heavy as a tonsil, like some hotel dweller, bored and weary,
like I'd wake up tomorrow to find that I didn't.

on the floor our wool socks mingle and alphabetize the carpet
in discarded curlicues; "spackle" is the word for this room, and
    the other one

where the window is (and the other TV)—rooms of whodunnit
walls designed to repel and keep the hair or semen or skin

bruised right into their forensic surfaces. jockeying for my hockey
gaze, these confines insist on the mania of those stuck

flipping through channels: how it seems more likely that tonight,
outside, in the woods by the highway where the dogs stare

I'll see some figure in the trees moving away from me, find
some woman, molested and dropped, more likely than the
    chance of spotting some

hockey hero in the halls, or that I'll sit in a chair on a porch
    in the rain
breathing the cool clear air, watching the neighbours come
    home late

(only to find I'm in a commercial for a nasal decongestant, or
living in a hotel with one small window and two TVs).

II. BEFORE OTHERS ARE THERE

INTERNATIONAL AND
NAVY CODE FLAG

I

INDIA — PHONETIC

Morse Code Symbol

BUCKSHOT FULLSTOP

In New Brunswick
they're pumping deer full of lead
                              type,

stuttering sentences through the trees,

rhyming buckshot fullstops.

(Estates are auctioning
their unwritten poems
into the arms of bargain hunters

      Kelsey, C&P, Kluge,
      Vandercook, Heidelberg,

      carted straight to the dump

but their type,
the fonts of old news,
are melted

      cast inkless into moulds
      of small lead balls,

rounded into imprecision.)

Holes,
punctuated road signs,
proclaim crude alphabets composed
of vocables: bullets
for speaking with animals.

IODINE

Iodine the point of entry:
vague memories of blood in the bathroom sink,
photographs,
the orange staining
and the sting, the roof-of-the-mouth smell:
acerbic and geranium.

More than the cut it is this—
deltas as
wrists and fingers, sink as
basin, basin as
watershed of something forgotten;
the warble of the fridge turning on.

Now. Clarity.

When we moved in with my mother's lover
the night of the fire on Monkland
we found a room of pictures,
walls of prints—

sienna shark on the beach
a woman my mother didn't know, laughing
two men dressed as Elvis sleeping on a couch, bottles
breasts and stomachs and thighs
an iron on a table, a dress
a hand in a sink stained dark

—square questions.

When we came back from black stairwells
carrying our apartment
the walls were white, only showing
for their surfeit of old pictures a faint bleeding
of push-pins, ferric
with the Montreal summer damp
and light through the blinds, slanted.

HONESTY

My father's mother grew Honesty
in her Alzheimer garden,
she dried flowers with dictionaries
I opened years later
her browned messages
couched in forgotten or misspelled words
as I thumbed through
my inheritance.

As a child in her house I would disappear
into a room with bouquets of dried Honesty
whose silver skin
held to light
were mother-of-pearl and birch paper
were the film on the stuffed bird's eye
and showed dark seeds
sliding
with the pressure of my thumbnail
an anagram I couldn't get
until one would split
the skin
slip out, well oiled and smooth
to my lips.

Checking the door, I would pocket it
and hope she wouldn't know
which had seeds
    and how many.

A MOOSE RUNNING ALONG THE HIGHWAY
OUTSIDE MEMRAMCOOK

no car of
canaries
we passed that moose lumbering
along the shoulder

the car beyond it already

and were left with marshpelt
dank and coloured by uproot
stump

the amble of deadly knees

it was a stone, this moose
a stone with a line tied to it and thrown into the water
thrown into the water with something on the other end
we couldn't remember
and the stone sank, and the line, and something sank
and the stone settled and murked up the water around it
and the line bent into the muddy bottom
and something was lost in the murk of it until that settled too
so it looked as though it had sat there

a long time

we sat there driving
and neither knew what we had been saying

A MOVEABLE

book, it has
crossed waters from Cuba
to Spain and back,
some iceberg plotting its course
under the greens
of distance and dulse, suspended

it is darker than ice is suspected of
and hidden, heavy, omitted.

This is about what is missing—

the book floats lightly as though travel carries no bags
only sequence, as though
the consequence of writing is what is written

—it is a book of times, then, hiding, of

these moments taken and guarded
like a plate of food
moments between stops, between meetings
moments waiting or waking, before others are there:

these rough, quick words,
so ugly from the pen.

ORTS: FEBRUARY EVENING

1.

coming down the escalator to the bus stop, someone standing
in the puddle of their shadow, shining from waxed cobbles; not
wearing my glasses—the way these second glances turn real

2.

the bus smells like
soy sauce,
pleather creaking

3.

running a beth for bath, a bath for beth;
she's sick, cold, slow

4.

walking rand in the storm, turning home against the wind; the
parking lot sheeted white, tire tracks
like they'd tried to plough the moon; the dog unsure of ice
cracking beneath her

5.

hand-setting a poem all week that's too long for my type: no Es
or Ts; orts; these scraps

6.

unfinished

TRADITIONAL DANCES FOR TOURISTS

blown tires watch the road as
sculpted crows

the cold deepens from sky into mood
the bath is not big enough to cover me with water

how I find you in others how I want them
for you

how raccoons die together a family
sequenced along the median, the smallest
a version
of going on

we've been watching travel programs
writing maps onto the walls, crossing out Australia

two months ago your brother told us he'd found a mouse had
    been living
in your brake pads

and circling the small islands

THE TENSION OF LOVE AND WINDOWS

outside, a passing car kindles the hills:
sets willow on willow on cornfield corduroy

the roll of lawn, the rise of stone farmhouse, grey
with dark in the thickened panes, leaded

there, between my back and the window
is the pull of your arms (I asked you to keep me from falling)

and the pattern of our love moves inward
to stomachs and knees, collarbones

angled to the tension of love in windows
lined by the reach of another car's light

TRANS–CANADA

When they built the trans-Canada
canal, the critics were everywhere—

citing the virtue of concrete over water,
asking why reinvent the wheel?

but the country mobilized
around an idea of slowtide cargo:

the Atlantics said they would conceive
the harbours, turn oceans to rivers,

Upper and Lower announced that they had already
done enough, with their lakes and waterways,

the Prairies set ploughs to furrow
a new bank of commerce, and

the West, though slow to agree to locks
through the Rockies, had to admit

the beauty of waterfalls
turned over.

III. GREEN TOMATOES

TYING THE RIVER

My father was an icefloe cowboy:
playing tug-of-war with the St. Lawrence breakup,
holding winter shaped like fish shacks and broken docks
from Montreal, shoreline and hands raw
with the pull of a springtime lasso;
his dinner getting cold.

This is how it started: that river must have rolled over,
caught his family and dragged them east
to the gulf, down north currents
to Nova Scotia. Here,
the sleeping kids were wrapped up
with the heirlooms when the house began to burn; outside
the neighbours and firetrucks marking the snow blue.

In the morning,
my father was a silverspoon woodsman:
tracking the night's ashes by firehose frost,
his axe hunting cutlery hidden in ice,
chipping the frozen plating off the silver
someone, my grandmother maybe, had dropped,
and casting his line
into the shafts of the family settings.

Later,
my father was a pick-up-stick sailor:
leaving Nova Scotia to come full circle
(if a circle can be a line of water)
running aground in the islands
of the same river's youth
where he found a stonehome,
a wooded one,
and then the cottage.

Here, I took a picture one May
of him out on the rocks he bought
because they reminded him of the coast
—that rare Atlantic edge of Ontario.

In it,
my father is a water pump dancer:
frozen where he stands on the rocks in the river
holding the intake above and around him in an arc
ready to throw
umbilical
so that when we flushed
the floor would rumble with the sound of it working.
The overcast sky coils
around him
the water unbroken. He's
tying the river,
tied, pulling in the lines of all these shores.

TO BETH, SLEEPING

the sky this weekend, the sky
and its blackberries dropping into your palm
at the moment that you put it there, your neck
stiff with driving is why I read to you
tonight until I could hear you breathing

in the morning I will stand outside
and wash your windows, the vertical lines of rain
stained through screening
that hold the yellow of the street lamps to them
while you sleep

BETH SEEKING POEMS

1.

a concordance of her name would suffice
beth glancing through my journal

the moments I allow her she browses
until she finds me writing her

there's no index to ease her sleuth, no book
of her name measured

accounted

the inevitable balance against all other words

2.

red, she says, should be my next poem

and I feel how a biographer must, with his subject still
living

is saffron the strands in their little plastic box
or the gold of their leaching?

and January tomatoes: are they red too?

3.

the days are spent thinking
elsewhere, the nights

on the hook
I keep my soul on

pulsing
    blue, beth,
    blue,

I hang my keys;
home from work.

GHAZAL OF JULY STORM

the smell of greenstalk tomatoes
on my fingers

the wind pressing into windows
testing their ripeness

the dog pacing
unsure of our night movement

the bamboo I've taken from the basement
to tie my plants

moments of love
talk that pauses into sleep

GREEN TOMATOES

this morning I unwrapped
the tomatoes from their newsprint:
old movies, old music, old editorial outrage
muffling them in an oiled soot of ink

two weeks ago, the morning after I picked them green,
I wrote

    the frost today
    each leaf rimed
    a geomancy of edges

and now some magic of old wrinkled language
has softened them into flesh—

the news has realized them red
and cups their round creases still,
folded into packets for the yellowing.

BELGRAVE AVENUE

Vannicola owned the block I grew up on
where crates appeared every year
in a parade song of trucks backing up:
stinking old Italy returning with grapes piled high
the cargo husks sitting for weeks on their stilts
doors swung, pavement sticky.

His soured wife stood at the till all day
her glasses framing her frown
her hair pushed up into yeasted loaves
her legs stoic behind cigarettes,
bus passes,
the fold-out hockey calendar that fit in your wallet.

Her store was where I learnt to hold out my hand and count
before bringing the change home

where salt seemed so cheap I bought two boxes
and they sat in the cupboard for years, sweating crusts

where the milk price was a calculus of three blocks to the next
    store
and my willingness to walk it

where I dropped off our rent and saw her take a pinch of twenties
while the till was open, her wallet perched beside it.

From there, I would walk the half block home
past square-metre fences to the highest apartment
where our balcony looked across flat roofs until
trees were tall enough to view, and down
on tomatoes and old bald men
brooding, shining,

and the woman across the alley threw cigarette butts from her
    window
scrolled messages waiting
to be picked up and read in secret.

Home, I would take the Canadiens schedule from the bag, walk
past my stepfather's darkroom where hockey was
already mixing into running water, find
the game on CBC radio,
past static, turning into night.

SAMUEL MARCHBANKS' DAUGHTER

Samuel Marchbanks' daughter
rubbed coal dust into her labia before
sneaking out the back for the night

she pulled her dad's beard
and gave him a snow job
making sure the cold got down his shirt

she wrote nasty letters to the editor
signed them from her teachers
their wives, their lovers

she showed the neighbours her ass
flattened into the panes of the kitchen window
as white as the February light

she walked the back alley in her fur coat
hanging her father's underwear
on everyone else's line.

PIAZZA DEL NETTUNO

If you were my gypsy
electric rock motorcycle guitar leather bicepped
father

and I were your uncomfortable daughter

I would cobblestone dance on our way through Bologna,
draw a crowd around us (speakers
on tripods, kickstand steady) tightly,
like an early father-daughter embrace, and

you would cringe a smile and play that fretboard
over the recording, make our audience sincere
with your grimace *we'll make money today, baby*
not fascinated, not embarrassed

but approving, like that, of my bends
and my nods to the music, you see:
my elbows and hips, my turns.

fearing a paucity of bees, I took up a zucchini flower and began to paint.

the male of the species is slim and upright, and I begin each morning by simply cutting a stem so that a pen is comparable in length; I tear the flesh from the flower, unwinding it from the golden arousal of the stamen within. this is my brush and with it, as ant and earwig, I enter and dawdle any open female.

the hero of these confessions is the zucchini itself.

I record this time so that you know the descent I have taken for you, what sex with species green, what trade I do with soil, light, and pollinating insect. all this so that I may form a firm fruit, catch the light with it,

and offer it for you to feel with care.

DOG SHOW BLUES   .

in March the pressure builds:
the fiercest of Ontario's competitors already down
in Florida, South Carolina,
to get the most of their season,

but the weekenders and spendthrifts and those never granted best
in show, are stuck practising that special podium lift, by scruff and
     by tail,
onto their coffee tables until the local arenas can shake the last
     skate:

from their northern couches
they watch the shows for the secret cadence of hand gesture
to transmit strangely in blue light
the signal for defeat.

THE LIFE AND EVOLUTION OF DUST BUNNIES

There's an algorithm, somewhere, that charts the lifecycles of
    dustbunnies
factors: when family comes to stay
rate of draft across floorboards
unsaid accounting of chores done, neglected
impact of holidays on curbside pickup.

There's a sine for what it means when they've grown too big:
confidently nesting in corners and under wool socks
on the dog's bed, breeding.

One can predict with some confidence the size and frequency
of said bunnies
the afternoon following the sweeping:
larger already, and bold,
drifting across a greater range
feeding from the slits between door and floor
and growing to sizes uncharted
in the widespread population that had come before.

The vector of their drift back to body masses
of a reasonable size, unnoticed and cohabiting,
is proven by the rattle of windows
by the scratching of dog
by the sex cycle, or frustration thereof

where t is time between
and the existence of brooms is a given.

A LOCAL HISTORY OF THE AIR CONDITIONER

In the window sits the air conditioner I railed against for months
until price and conviction dropped lower,
the heat higher and we bought it one day, the saving face
or grace being that you paid for it
with your card, divorced it from me.

All winter I've wrapped it in a blanket
because I refused to move the filing cabinet and fern
in order to take it from where it was bolted,
so it's provided a passive cooling of our apartment
and may have contributed to our keeping warm a bit more often.

And though I had imagined it to be the final product separating us
from our world, with its own seasons self-contained, now
I realize it ties us to the winter leaking in at its seams,
to the streetnoise and rainsound of spring, and even
to the heat of a lengthening summer we turn to machines to ignore.

THE TRIALS AND EXILE OF FRIDGES

In a world of narrow doorways
the fridge refuses to surrender
to the men
cursing
the counters built some time after
its reign began.

Sitting staunch
in the belief in its own freon,
it is a prisoner
of mouldings, frames, banisters,
of its own girth in the arms of two small men
telling each other to calm down
    fuck this, to call Steve
    no, to calm down
that this is a hell of a start to a Friday morning.

And the fridge,
cool but not cold to their efforts,
takes a step out onto the linoleum,
begins to reveal the world it's been hiding:
strata of tenants
where magnets and dog hair have eloped and settled.

And right there on my kitchen floor
it suffers the insult of these two men and their cheap act:
the removal of its doors, its heart and soul,
its mustard;
abandoned on the side porch for the cats to mark,
it is cared about by no one
but insurance men.

And through the pane
it can see the other fridge there,
new and nervous, hunching in tight
and not quite fitting the space
between the oven and the wall, but starting to purr.

TO THE POET WHO STOLE MY BOOTS, MY POEM.
for PB

Paul. recently, a friend met up with you in Victoria, bought one of your street poems. you probably didn't recall her as one of the women you followed around Dorothy's, haranguing with your stream of semi-conscious angry-victim verse, your over-the-bruised-lip-of-your-beer-bottle lip curl. I couldn't believe it when she sent it to me: a poem about someone stealing your shoes. I've told people about that night: how Dorothy felt some mix of charity and mischief in inviting you to her party, how you showed up damp and introverted, thirsty. when you were made to leave, I should tell you that the living room lost something. (it *was* a bit comic though, you fit the part so well: screaming indignation, going down the stairs backwards so you could piss up at your escorts, who were perhaps too proud with their task of kicking you out.) when I got up to go I had to ask for my boots, then describe them. Iain told me that he'd thought they were yours, gave them to you since they were so old, scuffed, poor. your real shoes were still sitting there, black leather too shiny for someone living in the park. Dorothy, in tears laughing, offered me a couple plastic bags to put over my socks, insisted on them actually. I sat on the arm of the couch by the door and she put them on my feet with elastic bands. the sound of them crinkling, their slip, bringing me back to winter boots as a kid. I wore them just past the stairs, then slapped down May St. in my wet wool socks, a metre long by the time I got home. all the way thinking: someday I'll write a poem about the street poet who stole my boots. only now you got that too.

M.

IV. COAL SMOKE DREAMS

MORNING CROW GHAZAL

The crow this morning has swallowed a kazoo
and croaks out his neighbourhood watchings,

angles his eye in hard malpeque circles,
cups you in his palm, flies and cuts you at the hinge;

the song a broken, silly one. Something
has opened the garbage bags onto the sidewalks;

I realize I have never imagined a crow as woman,
only a woman as crow. The rain has just started.

WOODPECKERS

a mother leans out her door
to watch for her kids,
coming home from school they
round the corner each day this time;

run, grab them—

your children will be blown away by this wind,
they'll salt their feet in the marshes,
lose all their hair to the low clouds
today, nesting birds,

the woodpeckers may find their ears.

WALKING DALLAS ROAD

where the stones hold their water
you can see the dogs have come
with their sticks
from the strait
darkly salted

a bird's wing in the
crabgrass cracks
closed with cold
too small
to lift the street from its perch
too small to lift the curb.

THREE PUMPKINS

1.

A day walking Petrie Island,
a farm of pumpkin fields orange, applebushels,
harvest ending in gourds too rough to eat.

2.

It's cold
the bus hasn't come—
a man is carrying
his eleventh-hour pumpkin
home,
where his children
with knives
are waiting.

3.

The morning after
I'm looking for dampened signs
of mischief;
the dog alert in the frost and leaves,
at the bottom of the street
the chainlink around Aberdeen
made medieval:
two impaled pumpkins
pike the gateposts—
winter is coming.

OAXACA POTATO

If the sky was as dark as Jesus' blood
then the streetlights were roman candles:

In Oaxaca, I confused a potato with the Pope
and offered him, wrapped in cheese and tinfoil,
to a woman sitting on the sidewalk with her children.

She may have been disappointed by this particular *Papa*,
or surprised, having already seen the Pope four times this life;
old hat.

For me, walking on,
this tuber like Catholicism: a mix of guilt with gilt,
though it was the firecrackers and dueling brass bands
that kept me up all night at the hotel
missing the better part of the celebrations.

Earlier, I'd managed to catch Jesus being paraded, buttressed
by crowd and cameras,
head hung in pride, arms splayed
transepts
handing out old world food.

MAZINAW/BON ECHO

We kayaked a lake
called writing
because the stones tell stories at eye level
  red turtle
  and cedar lichened to man
petroglyphs stained into land
that I could only hear through Purdy
(such a sensitive dead man)
laconic on CBC;

speaking these ochred drawings
I tested what my echo should be
but looked up to a climber's call:
  the ellipses of his loose footing
  coming to plug my eye
instead
plunking water nearby, rippling into rock
as we turned
our wakes to our bows
the dog left too long with friends on a beach;

above us,
across cliffs chalked with footholds
Scots' chisels once carved an epigram
into the granite rise
so hotel guests could see writing from land
and distinguish both
  'Old Walt'
cut into the name of the rock,
a history mortised there;

when we returned from the weekend
smelling woodfire clothing
with the scrawl of the lake
as long as we could
the phone was waiting
with my mother's quiet message
saying this was the weekend he died while camping
    her brother
can you call me;

but afterwards I thought
how neither of us spoke of coal smoke dreams or dying.

ENTROPY

how we hold burnt-out light bulbs to our ears, shake them:
how seeing sounds when it dies;

how we strip paper, paint, skin soft plaster walls:
how we know the atlas we make but not the place;

how I hear of friends travelling, reading, writing—
how I sit with my book, waiting; the house, waiting;

how I saw the moon tonight, our walk home, unfinished,
how I go on my own, not knowing my anger;

how I hold my glass between us those nights, my right hand,
enough to keep us sitting this way, the way we are.

SPRING THIS YEAR

we stand shocked, the tapping end of winter:
look to each other for the word that is woodpecker.

the pheasants lift from the marsh with their scream—
a dozen ladies pulling in their clotheslines as the rain begins.

but today is dry, and lonely, the dogs sitting there watching
as you reverse up the creek bed that was our driveway.

you leave, I've just returned, and there's a surface
to each day back, when the pattern isn't there yet. we wait for it

though we shouldn't, shouldn't wait for the pattern.
you leave, that's how it is, the dogs and I standing there.

QUEEN JANE APPROXIMATELY

a friend was over, saw the photograph of his dead father on my
    wall
and tried to speak without intent, to see where it would take him.

I've been guiding vines along the balcony railing each morning,
twisting them into forms of privacy, shade, where

I wait for the hour or moment that could allow drinking,
count the ice cubes: won't you come see me, aimless with heat?

each homecoming has the verglas
of our days apart, waiting.

on the bus from the interview, my throat like a tin lunchbox,
the tiredness of giving in, of working again, or planning to.

a woman on my street walks with a broom as her cane, its bristles
    flattened,
the pressure of always being pulled down.

FALL

Tonight the air has started through the vents:
the furniture takes on a new situation,

windows lose their vantage.

The woman next door has left her garden
razed like spring—
cool and green and low, a nose of flowers
she's cut to save face, to spite
her landlord and his many cousins who live downstairs,
the ones she's told you beat their wives,
the ones who hang sheets for curtains, floral patterns
upside down.

On the curb, someone's rotting crabapples
are finally gone, the cider smell
of breaking down settles into the sidewalk for winter.

Stalks and clutchings lie there, next door,
wait for Friday.

THE RELIQUARIES OF TREES

The reliquaries of trees
are sapling bone chainlink suspended,
lawn stump rooting pipe dry,
avenues tuning-forked to power lines,
patchwork arcanum of mountainside
(when seen from above)
and the sawdust cenotaphs of lumberyards—

where the woods mob in unruly,
try to see past the wind's shoulders
to where the kill site was,
crowd at the edge of roads laid to tell them
there's nothing to see here, nothing to see,
rub rooftops for a blessing, pray,
and queue for the time of their own haunting.

OWL SHAPED IN REEDS

What were those words in my head
a minute ago?
the silence of you leaving.

I feel I should pull people nearby
put their heads
    in the dip
between my shoulder and chest.

In Newfoundland tonight
you are mourning with your family
a man you sent postcards
the first time we saw mountains.

On the phone
you held me to the foghorn,
cupping the bay, and it told me.

I think of halyards from my summer nights
moaning with wind,
an owl shaped in reeds,
                bamboo,
                        hanging in my childhood—

toning out percussions
only the rain could taste.

V. HITCH

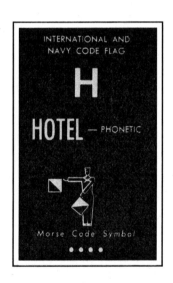

FIG. 1: PREFACE

when I first learnt to sail / we untied knots
after soaking our hands in buckets of ice / mimicking rivers
until we couldn't feel them

fingers stupid / thick
watching them / without the conduit of the spine

unresponsive lovers

FIG. 2: THE PREMISE OF TYING

to untie

FIG. 3: TYING THE KNOT

the history I have with loose ends / is not on the minds of my
    relatives
their euphemisms / misdirected to a sailor

who cannot leave
a knot
held fast

FIG. 4: HAGIOGRAPHY

Alexander of Macedon

a warning

FIG. 5: MOORING

the half-hitch is used for mooring
the round turn two half-hitch being / standard
dependable

easily untied

but still, you ask, isn't a two half-hitch / a hitch?
and there it is

FIG. 6: AEROMANCY

superstitious sailors used to tie three reefs
in a line / untie them
to call wind

with the third came hurricanes

a ligature of œs
a rosary of gales

this, from untying

FIG. 7: CHAINS

though we tie one on
together / it seems given

that the morning's eggs / coffee
will undo the knots in our stomachs
blocks in our heads

so we go / together
untying
but tying
untying

a chain

loving and drinking and loving / again

FIG. 8: EDITING

the sheepshank is a unique
knot / least for its name

its loops
and turns
like intestines
tightening

keeping a damaged line from splitting / the bight
bypassing frays

editing lines

/ shorter

FIG. 9: ALPHABET

in knotting some speak / an alphabet of bights
(a "b" looped over / a "d" looped under)
some count / in cordage
an abacus of movements

a Phœnician trading in language
for a musical scale:

bo / do / po / qo
bu / du / pu / qu

and   o/ver
but   u/nder

bees (bi) and dees (di) / pees (pi) and kews (kju)
like type pied /
out of sort

and   unadle to sqell
but   for semaphore

bravo delta / papa quebec

writing where the river / spills to
as my story

east / in lines
on water on paper

undoing

FIG. 10: FAST

knots in logs:
the record of speed

going faster / the goal
buying pre-stretched line so there couldn't be / a fraction
of give / in our rigging

knots / fast

knots by eye:
the guessing of wind

going faster / the goal

rough ridges at 7
intermittent caps at 12
whitecapping by 20
blowing stink at 25
honking beyond that / until
it was blowing the dog off the chain

knots / fast

strange, how the refrain is what we avoid / what we repeat
I never said I was going / too fast

FIG. 11: COMING TOGETHER

the sheet bend
is
two bodies / together

taut and twisted into each other
pulling

/ but temporary

then
coiled

FIG. 12: PAUSE

all this to say
there's an impasse on pulling this one off
smoothly

a stopper in the cam

I cannot make a knot
too gnarled for fingers
or marlin spike

too fast to be broken / and loosened

with fingers numbed
by cold / by heat

faltering

at heart lines

FIG. 13: STRANDED

these lines are woven / thick
twined with wind
and weight of water

to keep them

I should learn a sailor's eye / splice

roll it and make it long

the splice a knot / for keeping

fingers

stranded / together

FIG. 14: JUNE

I have found my book on tying / found
in a museum of the sea

in it / the Reeving Line
or Single Marriage Bend / it says

    is formed with a hitch on each side
    as illustrated, but it is not safe
    unless both ends are well seized
    to standing parts.

I am learning this / river /
with my fingers

threading
a hitch
on each side /

standing

a bad repoesy Mfg. Co. project

"at a certain point, Degas" was written after visiting an exhibit
of Degas bronzes at the Art Gallery of Ontario. The bronzes, of
horses in motion, were influenced by the pioneering photographer
Eadweard Muybridge.

The five 'science fictions' (originally released together as a
4lphabet Serial) are based on eponymous scientific theories.
"Smith's Invisible Hand" refers to Scottish proto-economist
Adam Smith (1723–90). Specifically, Smith's notion of the
"invisible hand" describes how an individual acting in self-
interest can be seen to promote the good of the greater society;
this, of course, within a frame of capitalism. "Heisenberg's
Uncertainty Principle" is based on a theory of German
physicist Werner Heisenberg (1901–76). It postulates that
it is not possible to know both the position and momentum
of a single particle at any one time. "Avogadro's Law" is an
exact representation of the true eventual story of the Italian
chemist, Amedeo Avogadro (1776–1856). Avogadro's law
suggests that an equal volume of gas will contain the same
number of molecules as another gas at the same temperature
and pressure, regardless of any differences in chemical or
physical properties. A "mole," or pure substance, is calculated
using "Avogadro's Number," 6.022×10^{23}. "Baer's Law (I and
II)" takes as its starting point Karl Ernst von Baer (1792–1876),
a Prussian-Estonian scientist of many disciplines. His first
law, of biology, states that embryos of a given species resemble
those of another (though not the adults of another) and that
the younger the embryos being compared, the greater their
potential resemblance—that development moves from simple
and homogenous to complex and distinct. His second law
relates to geography: it describes how a river's two banks will

erode asymmetrically, based on the earth's rotation and what hemisphere the river is on. "Starling's Law of the Heart" finds its inspiration in British physiologist, Ernest Henry Starling (1866–1927). Starling's law states that the heart's contractions are proportional to its intake: that it will beat based on the rate of blood return.

"a moose running along the highway outside Memramcook" owes an image to a great poem by John Steffler, "That Night We Were Ravenous."

"a moveable" is a poor attempt to present the biography of Ernest Hemingway's book, *A Moveable Feast.*

"confessions of a zucchini painter" partly borrows its title and tone from Thomas De Quincey.

"Samuel Marchbanks' daughter" concerns itself with the until-now neglected offspring of Robertson Davies' notorious diarist.

"queen jane approximately" takes its title from Bob Dylan's song.

"hitch" (originally published as a chapbook through above/ground press) takes its illustrations from the second, revised edition of *Knots, Splices, and Rope Work* by A. Hyatt Verrill (New York: The Norman W. Henley Publishing Co., 1917). "fig. 9: alphabet" hints at the form of Robert Kroetsch's earlier Can-lit sailor, the Sad Phœnician. The excerpt in "fig. 14: June" describing the marriage bend is from Raoul Graumont's *Handbook of Knots* (Cambridge, MD: Cornell Maritime Press, Inc., 1945).

ACKNOWLEDGEMENTS

The energy of the people behind the small presses and small
magazines of Canada is impossible to measure. I am humbled
to be publishing this book of poetry under the blewointment
imprint, and proud of Nightwood Editions for honouring
the small press tradition in this way. bill bissett, bp Nichol,
jwcurry and others proved that the vitality of Canadian letters
was in the small. I think it still is. So: to all the editors and
readers, the writers and designers of the small press and small
magazine—and, personally, to those I've worked with over the
years at *Arc Poetry Magazine*—I would like to offer my thanks
and encouragement: your work is important.

For the spaces in which this book was able to settle, begin,
form, I would like to thank *Arc Poetry Magazine*, *Carousel*, *CV2*,
Descant, *echolocation*, *The Fiddlehead*, *The Malahat Review*,
Modomnoc, *Prairie Fire Magazine* and *Rampike* for publishing
earlier versions of some of these poems. Special thanks also
go out to above/ground press and the 1928 press for their
fine chapbooks, keepsakes and support. I am grateful for the
work, largely unacknowledged but essential, that the staff of
Nightwood Editions has put into this book: my dream made
by so many hands.

To Silas White, in particular, for his knowledge, calm guidance and friendship I am grateful. Carleton Wilson's eye for quintessence and his love of typefaces, paper and careful design were more than I could ask for. To my many parents and sisters, my family, and those who have brought me into theirs, I owe everything: their belief in me and their love have made it all possible. Friends, whose thirst for ideas, for experience (or simply whose thirst), have brought me to many of the places to which these poems point: I am grateful for their love and companionship. To Triny Finlay, Anita Lahey and Rob Winger I owe a great deal: all early readers of a book that would not have been realized without their involvement, suggestions and friendship. I am indebted, also, to two later readers—Steven Heighton and Erín Moure were generous in their praise and gentle in their criticism, and both contributed significantly to these poems attaining a final state. To the readers to follow, my thanks for your time and trust.

And to beth, my first reader always, my thanks and my love: I could not, cannot, do it without you.

Neil Rough, 2006

ABOUT THE AUTHOR

Matthew Holmes is Chief Inspector of the bad repoesy Mfg.
Co. and publisher of the zine *Modomnoc*. He operates a small
printing press for publishing short poems and chapbooks,
including those in the "4lphabet Serials" series. Reviews editor
of *Arc Poetry Magazine*, his poetry and articles have appeared in
numerous journals and magazines. He lives in Sackville, New
Brunswick.